# HAPPY ANNIVERSARY

VANESSA CARDOSO WHELAN

PLAYWRIGHTS CANADA PRESS
TORONTO

First edition: October 2024
Printed and bound in Canada by Imprimerie Gauvin Ltée, Gatineau

Jacket photo © Jeremy Harnum
Author photo by Vaida Vaitkute Nairn

Playwrights Canada Press
202-269 Richmond St. W., Toronto, ON M5V 1X1
416.703.0013 | info@playwrightscanada.com | www.playwrightscanada.com



LIBRARY AND ARCHIVES CANADA CATALOGUING IN PUBLICATION
Title: Happy anniversary / Vanessa Cardoso Whelan.
Names: Cardoso Whelan, Vanessa, author.
Description: Includes some text in Portuguese.
Identifiers: Canadiana (print) 20240422422 | Canadiana (ebook) 20240422449 | ISBN 9780369105240 (softcover) | ISBN 9780369105257 (PDF) | ISBN 9780369105264 (EPUB)
Subjects: LCGFT: Drama.
Classification: LCC PS8605.A73 H37 2024 | DDC C812/.6—dc23

Playwrights Canada Press staff work across Turtle Island, on Treaty 7, Treaty 13, and Treaty 20 territories, which are the current and ancestral homes of the Anishinaabe Nations (Ojibwe / Chippewa, Odawa, Potawatomi, Algonquin, Saulteaux, Nipissing, and Mississauga / Michi Saagiig), the Blackfoot Confederacy (Kainai, Piikani, and Siksika), néhiyaw, Sioux, Stoney Nakoda, Tsuut'ina, Wendat, and members of the Haudenosaunee Confederacy (Mohawk, Oneida, Onondaga, Cayuga, Seneca, and Tuscarora), as well as Metis and Inuit peoples. It always was and always will be Indigenous land.

We acknowledge the financial support of the Canada Council for the Arts, the Ontario Arts Council (OAC), Ontario Creates, the Government of Ontario, and the Government of Canada for our publishing activities.

Canada Council for the Arts | Conseil des arts du Canada
ONTARIO ARTS COUNCIL
CONSEIL DES ARTS DE L'ONTARIO
an Ontario government agency
un organisme du gouvernement de l'Ontario
ONTARIO CREATES | ONTARIO CRÉATIF
Canada
Ontario

# PLAYWRIGHT'S NOTES

*Happy Anniversary* addresses gender-based violence as a collective story told by many women, with each voice contributing to a powerful narrative. Writing it was a challenging journey, but one I'm deeply grateful for. Hearing over thirty testimonials profoundly influenced the creation of this work.

The story sheds light on the diverse yet interconnected struggles faced by women in precarious situations. My hope is that this play contributes to ending gender-based violence, as it is unacceptable and change is imperative. I aspire for us to reach a place where such change becomes achievable.

I dedicate this play to all the courageous survivors who entrusted me with their stories, and to those still battling gender-based violence. You are not alone.

Thank you to all my family members, friends, and colleagues who supported and encouraged me throughout the writing process. I couldn't have done it without the love and patience from each of you. *Obrigada*!

# FOREWORD

## SOBIA SHAHEEN SHAIKH

Vanessa Cardoso Whelan has an exceptional capacity to use movement and creative impulse to evoke passion and connection. Vanessa is respected in the St. John's, Newfoundland & Labrador (NL), creative community for her mastery of multiple art forms—including dance, street and theatre performance, and playwriting. She brings many years of creative practice from NL and Brazil to her projects, giving her work artistic depth and breadth. As a fellow emerging playwright, I will always remember my admiration as I watched Vanessa's play *Saudade* at the 2023 Gros Morne Theatre Festival in Cow Head, NL, where she was able to deftly translate and embody the yearning and nostalgia of Brazilian "saudade." Nor can I forget her mesmerizing movement performance at the top of Signal Hill during Neighbourhood Dance Works's thirtieth Festival of New Dance, where she and musician Ana Luísa Ramos coloured the lively Newfoundland wind using dance, music, and bright fabrics from around the world.

*Happy Anniversary* was born out of strong and established theatre communities in St. John's and across Newfoundland & Labrador. The script began as part of TODOS Productions Writing Mentorship Unit with theatre creators Santiago Guzmán and Robert Chafe. In Newfoundland & Labrador, as in other parts of Canada, Indigenous, Black, Latinx, Asian, Arab, migrant, and other racialized theatre artists are determined to bring rich, yet-to-be heard stories of diverse people to the stage. The play is part of a new movement in playwriting and is a testament to the encouragement, dedication, and mentorship of NL-based theatre creators, especially racialized, migrant, and other historically minoritized artists.

The play is a compelling exploration of the themes of love, control, and empowerment within the context of intimate partner violence. At the heart of the play is Marta Dias, a woman ensnared in a twelve-year marriage that oscillates between moments of tenderness and yearning and episodes of violence and control. The narrative unfolds at a dinner table, a seemingly mundane setting that becomes a battleground for selfhood, love, and liberation. By skilfully juxtaposing scenes from the past and present, the audience is reminded of the pain and losses that Marta endures as she fights for her autonomy.

The use of music and dance throughout the play enhances the emotional depth of the narrative, making Marta's journey toward self-discovery and empowerment all the more poignant. Marta's love for dance is more than just a hobby; it is a form of expression and a metaphor for her longing for freedom. Dance and music throughout the play builds evocative tension, illustrating Marta's internal struggles and her moments of brief escape. The fluidity and grace of dance contrast sharply with the rigid control Carlos, her husband, imposes on her, highlighting the tension between confinement and liberation. The play's use of tango adds a dramatic effect, symbolizing the passionate yet perilous dance of their relationship, where each step can lead to connection or conflict.

While the story centres the relationship between Marta and Carlos, the script emphasizes the collective struggle against violence that many women and gender-diverse people face. The play's use of voice-overs that name and give voice to stories of women who have experienced brutality in their relationships show that Marta's struggle is not isolated but part of a broader, systemic social reality. The play also emphasizes the crucial roles that love and support of other women play in empowering women who experience intimate partner violence. Through shared experience and mutual support, the women in Marta's life—personified in the voice of Marta's sister—help her to reclaim herself, and, literally, *knit* new beginnings and renewal.

Vanessa Cardoso Whelan's *Happy Anniversary* reminds us of the transformative power of storytelling and the importance of uplifting minoritized perspectives. This play is a poignant call to action, urging us to confront the realities of intimate partner violence and to champion the voices of those who seek liberation and empowerment through artistic expression.

*Sobia Shaheen Shaikh is a creative writer, playwright, community organizer, and academic committed to using her work to challenge systemic injustice. Centring anti-racist, feminist, and social justice themes, her writing and artistic endeavours aim to illuminate marginalized voices, encourage dialogue, and inspire transformative action. Sobia lives in St. John's, Newfoundland, and serves as a member of several local and national organizations.*

# HELPLINE

If you are a victim or survivor of gender-based violence, know that it is not your fault, and you are not alone. Help is available.

Call 911 or the local police department if you fear for your safety or that of your children. You can also seek support in Canada from one or more of the following:

Assaulted Women's Helpline
www.awhl.org

Crisis Line
GTA 416.863.0511
Toll-Free 1.866.863.0511
Toll-Free TTY 1.866.863.7868
#SAFE (#7233) on your Bell, Rogers, Fido, or Telus mobile phone

Seniors Safety Line
Toll-Free 1-866-299-1011
TTY 1-866-299-0008

Fem'Aide
Pour les services en français, veuillez appeler FEM'AIDE
(Ligne de soutien pour femmes violentées)
1.877.336.2433
1.866.860.7082 (ATS)
www.femaide.ca

Talk 4 Healing
Culturally grounded helpline for Indigenous women.
1.888.200.9997
www.talk4healing.com

*Happy Anniversary* was first produced by TODOS Productions at LSPU Hall, St. John's, from April 27 to 30, 2023, with the following cast and creative team:

Marta: Ana Luísa Ramos
Carlos: Bruno Vinhas
Mel: Alicia Cruz

Director: Ruth Lawrence
Assistant Director: Vanessa Cardoso Whelan
Choreographer: Andrya Duff
Set and Prop Design: Meghan Greeley
Sound Design: Beto De La Paz
Costume Design: Nico Paulo
Lighting Design: Bob Stamp
Dramaturge: Sara Tilley
Stage Manager: Lina Makaga
Producers: Ana Pitol and Santiago Guzmán
Mentees: Cassondra Murray and Lisah Nsanzungwanko
ASL Interpreters: Heather Crane, Denika Philpott, Sheila Keats, and Dana Rideout

# CHARACTERS

Marta
Carlos
Mel

# SETTING

A dinner table with two chairs.

# PROLOGUE

*MARTA enters at the back of the theatre. A voice-over plays. One by one, women say their names. With each name MARTA takes a step closer to the stage.*

**VOICE-OVER:** Maria da Penha
Linda Santos
Diana Romero
Amanda Rose
Ana Soares
Chelsea Thompson
Vanessa Garcia
Laura Hall
Caroline Sullivan
Ruth Thomas
Marie Harris
Andrea Clark
Sarah White
Antonela Mattarazo
Karen Duff
Monica Matos
Aiko Tanaka
Patricia Ford
Jana Chada
Paula Duarte
Júlia Campos
Lori Taylor

Dai Nakamura
Paula Silva
Sandra Lopes
Melanie Lewis
Kathleen Kashindago
Ashley Whelan
Suzan Makame
Pascale Tremblay
Lisa O'Brien
Cortney Lee . . .

*The voice-over fades as* MARTA *stands down stage.*

**MARTA:** Marta Dias.

## SCENE 1: THE COUPLE

*MARTA and CARLOS explore tango movements throughout the scene, slowly moving in the direction of the dining area. "Bésame mucho" plays.*

**CARLOS:** Marta cooked a special dinner.

**MARTA:** To celebrate our anniversary.

**CARLOS:** It's just another day.

**MARTA:** Twelve years!

**CARLOS:** Marta is wearing a beautiful dress and an apron.

**MARTA:** We are not going out.

**CARLOS:** But Marta wants to feel pretty.

**MARTA:** Carlos doesn't like to go out anymore.

**CARLOS:** Marta is twelve years younger than Carlos.

**MARTA:** Carlos is an accountant. He works fourteen hours a day.

**CARLOS:** Marta doesn't work outside the house—

**MARTA:** Carlos doesn't let Marta work outside the house.

**CARLOS:** Marta likes to dance. She takes tango lessons with her sister, Mel.

**MARTA:** Carlos doesn't like to dance but he always watches Marta's classes.

**CARLOS:** Marta takes good care of the house, but lately she has been forgetful.

**MARTA:** Carlos plays soccer with co-workers once a week.

**CARLOS:** Marta knits blankies and donates them to the children's hospital.

**MARTA:** Carlos and Marta don't have kids.

*A beat.*

Carlos is funny and charming at work.

**CARLOS:** Marta used to work at the cafeteria Café Corazon.

**MARTA:** Where Carlos still goes for lunch every day. One day Carlos invited Marta for a drink.

**CARLOS:** Marta said yes.

**MARTA:** Soon they became husband and wife.

*The song ends sharply.*

# SCENE 2: JUST ANOTHER DAY

*CARLOS is back from work; he takes off his suit and hands it to MARTA.*

**MARTA:** *Como foi seu dia?*

*CARLOS looks at his phone, not paying attention to MARTA.*

**CARLOS:** Busy.

**MARTA:** Oh, mine was good. I—

**CARLOS:** Did you check with my mom about next Saturday at church?

**MARTA:** She said—

**CARLOS:** Yes or no?

**MARTA:** Yes.

**CARLOS:** I'm hungry. Is supper ready?

*MARTA finishes the final details of setting the table.*

**MARTA:** Yes.

*A beat.*

So, I read that the twelfth-year anniversary gift is silk.

CARLOS *is looking at his phone, not paying attention.*

That means luxury and comfort, so I made—

**CARLOS:** Where is my drink?

**MARTA:** Just a sec.

**CARLOS:** Did you wash my soccer shirt? I need it for tomorrow.

**MARTA:** Oh shit.

**CARLOS:** Yes?

**MARTA:** I will do it.

**CARLOS:** Did you forget it again?

MARTA *gives* CARLOS *his whisky.*

**MARTA:** No, of course not.

**CARLOS:** What's on your mind these days?

MARTA *sips her wine. There is an awkward silence.* MARTA *looks at* CARLOS *as he downs his whisky.*

## SCENE 3: FIRST DATE

*"Los cosos de al lao" plays.*

**MARTA:** Carlos took Marta for dinner at La Maison . . . Nice place.

**CARLOS:** Marta was a bit shy at first.

**MARTA:** Carlos was interested in Marta's story.

**CARLOS:** Marta wanted to know more about Carlos.

**MARTA:** Carlos looked at Marta with passion.

**CARLOS:** Marta really liked Carlos.

**MARTA:** Carlos was a gentleman, sweet and smart.

**CARLOS:** Marta laughed at Carlos's jokes.

**MARTA:** Carlos was in love with Marta.

**CARLOS:** Marta will be Carlos's wife.

# SCENE 4: PHONE CALL

*MARTA is on the phone with MEL. MEL is busy with her four-year-old son Pedro.*

**MARTA:** *Oi, Mel! Como vai?*

**MEL:** *Hi, Martinha, bem e você?* Tell me everything.

**MARTA:** I think I'm in LOVE!

**MEL:** Okay . . .

**MARTA:** He took me to La Maison. We talked a lot—he's so sweet.

**MEL:** Sounds good. What else? Shii, Pedro.

**MARTA:** *Ai*, Mel, I can't wait to see Carlos again and introduce him to you.

**MEL:** When is the next date?

*(to Pedro)* Yes, yes.

**MARTA:** Next Saturday, he said that his mom wants to meet me. I'm so nervous.

**MEL:** She will love you. Oh and Pedro has more drawings for your walls, sorry. I can bring them next time I visit.

**MARTA:** *Adoro!* Tell him I want another dinosaur.

**MEL:** Okay, *beijos, mana.* I have to go. Let's talk later, okay? *Tchau.*

**MARTA:** *Beijo, tchau.*

## SCENE 5: WE SHOULD CELEBRATE

*MARTA and CARLOS are sitting at the dinner table.*

**MARTA:** So, we should celebrate our day.

**CARLOS:** I gave you a card this morning.

**MARTA:** Yeah, but I mean some dates are special—remember our first-year anniversary?

**CARLOS:** What about it?

**MARTA:** You took me to that fancy restaurant, the same place we had our first date, remember?

**CARLOS:** Yes, and you told me that it was your first time eating risotto.

**MARTA:** I didn't really like it, but the place was beautiful.

**CARLOS:** Yes.

**MARTA:** The night was so clear and warm . . . Long time since we have been anywhere, so we should go some day.

**CARLOS:** Why? To post on fucking Facebook?

**MARTA:** That or to get out of the routine.

**CARLOS:** I like having a routine. Coming home after a stressful day is part of it. You should know.

**MARTA:** It would help you to relax, see people.

**CARLOS:** I see people all day. Why did you share this?

*He shows* MARTA *his phone.*

**MARTA:** Because she's missing.

**CARLOS:** You don't know the person: delete it.

**MARTA:** It's important to share. It's another woman missing.

**CARLOS:** You sharing it won't change anything: delete it.

**MARTA:** I think about the families . . . Must be a nightmare, not knowing where your loved ones are, and the person too, oh my.

**CARLOS:** So you should celebrate that you are here! You have all this and don't even need to go out and work. Luxury and comfort . . . I'm doing my part.

**MARTA:** Oh yeah, you're doing your part.

**CARLOS:** What is that? Is it not enough?

**MARTA:** *Sim*, it is, but . . .

**CARLOS:** But?

**MARTA:** For once you and I should do something, like eat out.

**CARLOS:** You're ungrateful.

**MARTA:** I'm thankful, Carlos, but I was thinking when—

**CARLOS:** Oh, you're thinking?

**MARTA:** Yes, I was thinking, when was the last time we—

**CARLOS:** There you go again. You know I work, right? And on weekends I need a break, and we have church, and Mom. That's our time together, family time.

**MARTA:** I appreciate all that, but I miss our dates. We need time as a couple too.

# SCENE 6: DATE AT CARLOS'S PLACE

*"La cumparsita" plays.*

**MARTA:** Carlos invited Marta over to his place.

**CARLOS:** Marta was so gorgeous that night!

**MARTA:** Carlos took Marta's jacket and helped Marta with her shoes.

**CARLOS:** Marta was wearing a red dress.

**MARTA:** Carlos offered Marta a glass of wine.

*Sim*, please.

Carlos served Marta.

*A toast:*

**CARLOS & MARTA:** *Saude!*

**CARLOS:** Marta had her hair down. She has beautiful hair.

**MARTA:** Carlos made pasta.

**CARLOS:** Marta was totally surprised that Carlos could cook. Marta helped Carlos clean the kitchen after supper.

**MARTA:** Carlos left a mess.

*MARTA laughs.*

**CARLOS:** Marta has two roommates. Her family lives in another city.

**MARTA:** Carlos takes care of his mother. His dad died when he was ten.

**CARLOS:** Marta said that she wants to have a family.

**MARTA:** Carlos told me he wants to be a dad.

**CARLOS:** Marta met Carlos's mom.

**MARTA:** Carlos touched Marta's face and smiled.

**CARLOS:** Marta kissed Carlos.

**MARTA:** Carlos said "I love you."

## SCENE 7: PHONE CALL

*MARTA is on the phone with MEL.*

**MARTA:** *Oi*, Mel! How is everything?

**MEL:** Hi, good! How was the date?

**MARTA:** It was magical!

**MEL:** Where did you go?

**MARTA:** To his place. His mom lives next door.

**MEL:** Have you met her? How is she?

**MARTA:** Yes, she's very sweet. She dropped by to say hi, and then left us alooneee!! She said that she can't wait to have a daughter-in-law.

**MEL:** Oh, okay. I'm not sure if I want to know details . . . *Ai!* Is he gooood?

**MARTA:** I love him, Mel. And yes! No details . . .

**MEL:** Wow! Love . . . It's been what? A month?

**MARTA:** *Ai*, Mel, stop! You know me, *sou romantica* . . .

**MEL:** Hmm . . . When are you coming home? You left a bunch of stuff here.

**MARTA:** I know! Soon. I miss Mom and Dad too . . . Should I bring Carlos with me?

**MEL:** Yes, I can't wait to meet him.

**MARTA:** If he doesn't propose . . . Maybe I will.

**MEL:** *Ta loca!* Don't be crazy . . . Don't be like me, believing in a fairy tale.

**MARTA:** I know. Okay, I got to go, my break is over.

**MEL:** Okay, *mana*, don't rush things. I don't want to see you with a broken heart like me . . . I'm good now, but you know, it was hard.

**MARTA:** You have a precious boy now, that's what matters.

**MEL:** That's true . . . I'm happy for you, *mana. Tchau, beijos.*

**MARTA:** *Beijos, tchau.*

## SCENE 8: THE ARGUMENT BEGINS

**CARLOS:** You're so annoying! "When was the last time we did something special?" You know we can't be out much. Mom could need us at any time.

**MARTA:** Your mom is fine, Carlos.

**CARLOS:** How do you know?

**MARTA:** I'm with her basically all day.

**CARLOS:** Mom likes to have company, you know that.

**MARTA:** And at night she has the nurse, even though she doesn't really need one.

**CARLOS:** Are you a doctor now?

**MARTA:** I'm just tired, Carlos, and I'm not asking for much.

**CARLOS:** Tired of what?

**MARTA:** Of being here all day. Doing the same things.

**CARLOS:** You don't know how many women would be happy here, living your life.

*MARTA looks at CARLOS. She doesn't agree.*

## SCENE 9: NOT A HAPPY LIFE

*CARLOS and MARTA are outside together after a church service. Church bells ring.*

**MARTA:** The service was refreshing, don't you think?

**CARLOS:** Maybe for you. Let's go.

**MARTA:** Are you okay? I didn't mean to upset you, sorry.

*MARTA waves to someone.*

*Tchau*, Maria.

*CARLOS waves as well, smirking.*

**CARLOS:** Why did you disagree with me in front of everyone?

**MARTA:** I was giving my opinion.

*(to someone)* See you next week.

*CARLOS waves to some other people.*

**CARLOS:** You should just not say anything.

**MARTA:** Sorry if my opinion is different from yours.

**CARLOS:** That was disrespectful. People will think that you wear the pants in our house.

*MARTA waves to another person.*

**MARTA:** Let's talk later—and who cares?

*CARLOS storms off to the parking lot.*

**CARLOS:** I care!

**MARTA:** Carlos, can you wait?

**CARLOS:** Walk home.

**MARTA:** What? Carlos. I'm sorry.

**CARLOS:** Next time, think before speaking.

*MARTA waves to another person as CARLOS turns to leave.*

**MARTA:** *Tchau*, Sarah.

*CARLOS slams the car door shut and races out of the parking lot.*

*MARTA stands there, alone.*

## SCENE 10: SAD SITUATION

*MARTA calls MEL.*

**MARTA:** *Oi*, Mel, *tudo bem*?

**MEL:** Yes, and you?

**MARTA:** Not really . . .

**MEL:** What now?

**MARTA:** Carlos was angry with me last night after church. He left me there.

**MEL:** What an asshole!

**MARTA:** I walked all the way home, in heels.

**MEL:** That's crazy . . . Was his mom there?

**MARTA:** No, she just goes on Sundays now.

**MEL:** You have to do something about it.

**MARTA:** He hasn't apologized yet, but it was my fault.

**MEL:** He's getting worse! And you still protect him!

**MARTA:** I don't know what to do.

**MEL:** You should start to save some money and leave him.

**MARTA:** What? No, Mel, how am I going to do that?

**MEL:** How long will you live like that?

**MARTA:** *(sad, unsure, confused)* He will change.

**MEL:** When?

**MARTA:** I love him . . .

**MEL:** We have to figure something out. I'm glad you're fine . . . but he's a monster.

**MARTA:** I got to go. His mom is calling me.

**MEL:** Okay, take care, *mana*, I love you . . .

*Transition. The voice-over continues, with more survivors speaking their names:*

**VOICE-OVER:** Chelsea Thompson
Vanessa Garcia
Laura Hall . . .

# SCENE 11: THAT'S WHY WE FIGHT

**CARLOS:** You don't know how easy you have it. I've provided you with everything from the beginning.

**MARTA:** Yes, Carlos, I know that.

**CARLOS:** I can't understand you. We're fine a minute ago, and then you have to disagree with me.

**MARTA:** I'm trying to have a—

**CARLOS:** That's why we fight. Even Mom said that you're acting weird.

**MARTA:** Oh yes, she knows everything.

**CARLOS:** Every mother knows what's best for their kids—you wouldn't know that.

*MARTA pours herself more wine.*

**MARTA:** Really?

**CARLOS:** Maybe if you were a mother, you would have less time to think such shit.

**MARTA:** Sometimes I'm glad I'm not the mother of your child.

**CARLOS:** You will regret that.

**MARTA:** God knows what's best.

**CARLOS:** I don't know what's in your head. You're changing.

*MARTA's phone beeps: a text message.*

I don't like it—

*It beeps again.*

*MARTA checks her phone.*

**MARTA:** People change, Carlos.

*It beeps again.*

**CARLOS:** I don't like it. Who is texting you?

**MARTA:** Mel.

**CARLOS:** I bet she's putting things in your head again.

*MARTA texts back.*

**MARTA:** Why do you think that?

**CARLOS:** First was that dance shit. Why did she move here? She should have stayed in that shithole where you came from.

**MARTA:** You don't need to offend my family.

**CARLOS:** You and your family should thank me.

*MARTA texts.*

**MARTA:** Thank you for what? Don't be ridiculous. Money isn't everything.

**CARLOS:** What does she want?

**MARTA:** Nothing. She just sent me a picture of Pedro.

**CARLOS:** Give me your phone . . .

*MARTA passes her phone to CARLOS.*

Picture of Pedro . . . Do you have to tell Mel everything?

**MARTA:** She's my sister and the only friend I have left.

**CARLOS:** Look at this: "I want to go but Carlos won't let me . . . "

**MARTA:** Jesus, are you going to read all my texts?

**CARLOS:** Does she know why I don't like to go to parties? Does she?

# SCENE 12: WANNA DANCE?

*A party with* CARLOS*'s co-workers.* MARTA *dances, carefree, like no one is watching.*

*A samba plays.*

CARLOS *is watching at* MARTA*—she's drunk.*

**MARTA:** What? Relax.

**CARLOS:** We probably should go.

**MARTA:** Now?! But the party just started.

**CARLOS:** Marta.

MARTA *stands up and starts to dance again.*

**MARTA:** I wanna dance! Who wants to dance with me? Paul, please, my husband doesn't like to dance!

CARLOS *laughs nervously.*

**CARLOS:** Yes, Paul, go dance with her.

**MARTA:** Yeah! Let's samba.

*MARTA dances again like nobody's watching. She loses her balance.*

*CARLOS helps MARTA.*

**CARLOS:** You're embarrassing me. Let's go.

**MARTA:** Am I embarrassing you? Haha, sorry. I am SORRY.

*CARLOS grabs her arm.*

**CARLOS:** Let's go NOW!

**MARTA:** No!! I don't want to go yet! You go! I can get a ride with Paul.

**CARLOS:** *(under his breath)* You will pay for that.

**MARTA:** You can't see me happy.

**CARLOS:** Shut up, let's go!

*CARLOS and MARTA glide through a tango transition movement.*

*At home.*

I want to see you dance now.

**MARTA:** I'm tired.

**CARLOS:** Dance for me like you're dancing with Paul.

**MARTA:** Carlos, please stop! I'm not in the mood.

**CARLOS:** Oh, now you're tired, but you weren't tired making a fool of yourself.

*CARLOS starts to take off MARTA's dress.*

**MARTA:** Carlos, no, I don't wan—

**CARLOS:** I know you enjoy it.

**MARTA:** No, stop. I don't want to.

**CARLOS:** I don't fucking care—you're my wife!

*MARTA freezes.*

## SCENE 13: MORNING SUNSHINE

*CARLOS acts like nothing has happened. He has a cup of coffee for MARTA. Birds sing.*

**CARLOS:** Good morning, sunshine . . . How did you sleep?

**MARTA:** Okay . . . I'm sorry about last night. I had too much wine.

**CARLOS:** Yeah, you need to learn to control yourself. It wasn't the first time.

**MARTA:** It won't happen again, sorry.

**CARLOS:** It was a shit show.

**MARTA:** I'm sorry.

*CARLOS kisses MARTA's forehead.*

**CARLOS:** Mom already asked where you were. I said we had a late night . . . *Tchau*, I love you . . .

*CARLOS brings a scarf for MARTA.*

Wear a scarf. You have some love marks on your neck.

*CARLOS leaves.*

*"Pasional" plays.*

MARTA *looks at herself in the mirror of a vanity. She's sad and ashamed.* MARTA *dances/moves by herself. This is a moment of realization: she's not happy and the man she loves and trusts is not a good person.*

# SCENE 14: MEL IS THE PROBLEM

*CARLOS continues drinking and scrolling through MARTA's phone.*

*The phone beeps: a TikTok notification.*

**CARLOS:** You have TikTok now?

**MARTA:** It's just an app. I don't use it.

**CARLOS:** Mel is brainwashing you with ideas from that stupid feminist book she gave to you. *Women Walking with Dogs*, or *Wolves* . . . Something stupid like that.

**MARTA:** Do you really think that?

**CARLOS:** You're knitting like crazy, she convinced you to do that tango shit—even I go to that fucking thing to watch you dancing with that guy. I see the way he holds you.

**MARTA:** Fernando is gay, for God's sake.

*CARLOS puts MARTA's phone on the table.*

**CARLOS:** And you want me to believe that?

**MARTA:** You don't need to go just to watch.

**CARLOS:** Now you don't want me to go.

**MARTA:** It's better you stay here having your quiet time.

**CARLOS:** I know what you want—you want another man!

**MARTA:** He's gay, Carlos!

**CARLOS:** I'm not enough for you.

**MARTA:** Can you hear what you are saying?

**CARLOS:** Yes, because I'm right. I see the way you act there.

# SCENE 15: TANGO CLASS

*MARTA sings, getting ready for tango class.*

**MARTA:** *Bésame, bésame mucho . . . bésame mucho . . .*

**CARLOS:** Marta was getting ready for tango class.

**MARTA:** *Como se fosse essa noite a última vez . . .*

*CARLOS grumbles.*

**CARLOS:** Marta was singing that foolish song.

**MARTA:** Carlos was looking at Marta with that jealous look.

**CARLOS:** *(jealously)* Marta was brushing her hair.

**MARTA:** Carlos was drinking.

**CARLOS:** Marta was getting all pretty, to dance with Fernando.

**MARTA:** Carlos snatched the brush from Marta's hands.

**CARLOS:** *(angrily)* Marta is not going today.

**MARTA:** Carlos, please! No!

*CARLOS and MARTA glide through a tango transition movement.*

# SCENE 16: WRONG NUMBER

*MARTA is on the landline with MEL.*

**MEL:** *Oi, Martinha, tudo bem?*

**MARTA:** Hi, Mel. I'm okay, *e você*?

**MEL:** Your voice is sad.

*MARTA tries to hide that she's not okay.*

**MARTA:** Nothing to worry about.

**MEL:** Why did you miss tango last night? I texted and called your cell.

**MARTA:** Carlos broke my phone.

**MEL:** Jesus! Are you okay, *mana*?

**MARTA:** I don't know what to do. I'm tired—

**MEL:** *Filho da puta!*

**MARTA:** He had a hard day at work, and I was singing . . . I should stop with the classes.

**MEL:** No, Marta!

**MARTA:** It will be better for us, Mel.

**MEL:** NO! That's the only thing you do for yourself. You have to stop doing what he tells you to do.

**MARTA:** He just wants what's best for us.

**MEL:** Let me call the police.

**MARTA:** No, Mel . . . You know when someone loves you too much . . . They do things to show their love.

**MEL:** Exactly. That's not love, Marta. That's not how you show love.

*CARLOS enters the room.*

**MARTA:** Gotta go.

**CARLOS:** *(suspicious)* I forgot my wallet. Who's on the phone?

*MARTA hangs up the phone.*

**MARTA:** Nobody.

**CARLOS:** Why did you hang up?

**MARTA:** Wrong number.

*Transition. The voice-over continues, with more survivors speaking their names:*

**VOICE-OVER:** Antonella Matarazzo
Karen Duff
Monica Matos . . .

# SCENE 17: I DON'T RECOGNIZE YOU

*CARLOS is standing behind MARTA's chair.*

**CARLOS:** I just want to come home and have a quiet time, and you have to start. I celebrate things my way, you should know better.

**MARTA:** *(concerned)* Okay, Carlos, let's try to have a nice night.

**CARLOS:** When we met, I thought that you would never be like that. Talking back, complaining. Where is that perfect woman? I don't recognize you sometimes.

**MARTA:** Same here.

# SCENE 18: SUMMER DAY LOVE BIRDS

*"Poema" plays.*

**CARLOS:** It was a beautiful summer day.

**MARTA:** Carlos took Marta for ice cream.

**CARLOS:** Marta had a day off.

**MARTA:** Carlos had plain vanilla ice cream.

**CARLOS:** Marta ordered mango with chocolate and sparkles. Marta and Carlos went for a stroll in the park.

**MARTA:** Carlos cleaned Marta's ice cream moustache.

**CARLOS:** Marta looked so beautiful.

**MARTA:** Carlos was dressed totally differently from what he wears to work.

**CARLOS:** Marta wore a long dress with flowers, very colourful.

**MARTA:** Carlos told Marta about his family. He has a younger brother who is married and has two kids.

**CARLOS:** Marta has one sister, two brothers, and three nephews. Marta's favourite colour is red.

**MARTA:** Carlos was a handsome and charming guy . . .

**CARLOS:** Marta's smile was contagious . . . lovely eyes.

**MARTA:** Carlos put a flower in Marta's hair.

**CARLOS:** Marta smiled shyly.

**MARTA:** Carlos held Marta's hands.

**MARTA & CARLOS:** They were happy.

## SCENE 19: CARLOS, DON'T, LET IT GO

**CARLOS:** I work so hard to give you the perfect life.

**MARTA:** *(concerned)* Oh yeah, perfect life.

**CARLOS:** You started and now you will listen.

**MARTA:** I started?

**CARLOS:** I was stupid to believe that you were the one for me. You're not. You're a piece of shit just like Mel.

**MARTA:** What does Mel have to do with this?

**CARLOS:** Because she puts things in your head.

**MARTA:** Oh yeah!

**CARLOS:** She doesn't have a man to straighten her out, to guide her: a woman needs a man.

**MARTA:** Yes, like a fish needs a bicycle.

**CARLOS:** Smartass.

**MARTA:** Yes, I am.

CARLOS: I see how you two act together.

MARTA: You're crazy!

CARLOS: You wanna see crazy! You look like a different person when you're with her.

MARTA: Are you jealous of Mel now?

CARLOS: I'm not fucking jealous. I just don't trust her.

## SCENE 20: PLANS

*MARTA is on the phone with MEL.*

**MARTA:** Hi, *mana*, I have a new phone, we can text again. Carlos apologized.

**MEL:** Asshole . . . How are you doing?

**MARTA:** Fine, but I feel like I'm doing something wrong behind his back.

**MEL:** Do you have another plan?

**MARTA:** No, but it feels like stealing. If Carlos discovers it.

**MEL:** You're not doing anything wrong. It might help you some day.

**MARTA:** I'm just afraid.

**MEL:** You can't only count on Carlos. The "everything" he "gives" you means nothing to me. I'm worried about you.

**MARTA:** He loves me, Mel. He's not going to kill me. Jesus.

**MEL:** Are you reading the book?

**MARTA:** Yes, it's helping me. *Obrigada.*

**MEL:** I have another one for you. I can bring it to tango.

**MARTA:** Good, and I will bring more blankies for you.

**MEL:** Okay, *mana*, I got to go. Keep knitting your way out . . . Call or text any time.

**MARTA:** Okay, *obrigada, tchau.*

*Transition. The voice-over continues, with more survivors speaking their names:*

**VOICE-OVER:** Lori Taylor
Dai Nakamura
Paula Silva . . .

## SCENE 21: YOU RUINED MY NIGHT

**CARLOS:** You're worse than Mel.

**MARTA:** I don't say those things about your family.

**CARLOS:** Because there is nothing bad about my family.

**MARTA:** Yeah, you're right.

**CARLOS:** I don't like your attitude.

*MARTA grabs her phone.*

Mel is a slut but at least she's a mother. God blessed her with Pedro and *Tio* Carlos is here to be a model for him.

**MARTA:** Pedro has a father. They don't live together, but he has a father.

*A beat.*

**CARLOS:** Why do you do that? Ruin my night.

"Pedro has a father" . . . I'm not a father and who's fault is that?

# SCENE 22: MARTA IS PREGNANT

*A song by Bach plays.*

CARLOS *and* MARTA *are happy with the news.*

**CARLOS:** Is it for real? *Vou ser pai?*

**MARTA:** Yes, I'm pregnant! Don't tell anyone yet, not even your mom, you know this is our fourth time trying.

**CARLOS:** Last time the doctor said that happens more than we think. You have to stop drinking wine—my boy needs to grow healthy.

**MARTA:** I know, Carlos, and we don't know if it's a boy or a girl.

**CARLOS:** Got to be a boy to go play soccer with Daddy. He will be the next soccer star!

**MARTA:** Oh my God, Carlos, it is not even a human yet.

**CARLOS:** Of course it is.

**MARTA:** I have an appointment next month.

*CARLOS puts his hand on MARTA's belly. A moment of stillness.*

*Pause.*

*A transition song plays.*

# SCENE 23: MARTA HAD ANOTHER MISCARRIAGE

**CARLOS:** How are you feeling?

**MARTA:** A bit better.

**CARLOS:** Mom made some soup for you.

**MARTA:** I don't understand. I was taking care of myself . . .

**CARLOS:** Try not to think.

**MARTA:** *(pensive, sad)* I'm sorry. Should we keep trying? I want to give you a child.

**CARLOS:** Just rest. Maybe it is not the time. God knows what is best.

## SCENE 24: MARTA TALKS WITH MEL

**MEL:** *Oi*, I'm so sorry.

**MARTA:** *(sad) Oi, obrigada.*

**MEL:** How can I help you? Do you want me to go there? Mom can look after Pedro.

**MARTA:** No, I will be okay. Maybe I'm not meant to be a mom, just an auntie.

**MEL:** You're a great auntie and will be a good mom one day.

**MARTA:** I was feeling so good.

**MEL:** Pedro wants to give you another drawing.

**MARTA:** He's so sweet . . . Did you tell him?

**MEL:** Yes . . . sorry.

**MARTA:** That's fine. *Saudades de vocês.*

**MEL:** We miss you too. If you need anything please let me know.

**MARTA:** *Obrigada, beijos . . . Tchau.*

**MEL:** Take care.

*Transition. The voice-over continues, with more survivors speaking their names:*

**VOICE-OVER:** Kathelenn Kashingado
Ashley Whelan
Diana Romero . . .

## SCENE 25: ANGER BUILDS UP

**MARTA:** It isn't anyone's fault, Carlos.

*CARLOS grumbles and and downs another drink.*

**CARLOS:** I can't believe how stupid I was . . . "I want to do this, let's go out of the routine." Nothing is good enough for you! Nothing! Why am I not enough?

**MARTA:** Carlos, I'm sorry, let's finish supper.

**CARLOS:** Listen to me. I don't want to come home and listen to your bullshit anymore.

**MARTA:** I understand, please.

**CARLOS:** I should be the one who's tired. You have no idea about the shit I have to deal with all day . . . all the bullshit I have to put up with in my job, being worried about Mom.

**MARTA:** Your mom will be here soon for dessert. Please calm down.

**CARLOS:** You don't tell me to calm down.

# SCENE 26: KNITTING AWAY

*MARTA and MEL are on the phone.*

**MEL:** Hi. I sold the last ten blankies. Can you knit a dinosaur?

**MARTA:** I can try. Carlos noticed that I'm kitting more.

**MEL:** Oh yeah, and?

**MARTA:** I said that we are donating some to the hospital as well . . . I don't like to lie.

**MEL:** You're not lying. We are still donating part of it.

**MARTA:** You're right. I'm just scared, I think.

**MEL:** How are things these days?

**MARTA:** You know . . . Some days are good, mostly church days, and some days . . . I'm just quiet, knitting away.

**MEL:** We are here for you, *mana*.

**MARTA:** I know . . . *Obrigada*.

**MEL:** You're doing great. The blankies are selling good.

**MARTA:** I have twenty more for you. I still don't like to think that I will use this money like that.

**MEL:** *Entendo, mana*, but sometimes life puts us in some weird situations . . .

**MARTA:** Don't we have enough?

**MEL:** If you two get a divorce, you already have at least a bit of money saved to rent a place to start over, keep knitting . . . That's your way out.

**MARTA:** I will bring them to tango.

*CARLOS enters.*

**CARLOS:** Who is on the phone?

**MARTA:** *(a bit nervous)* Okay, *obrigada, mana. Tchau.*

**MEL:** *Eu e Pedro te amamos*, okay! Take care, *beijos*.

*MARTA hangs up.*

**CARLOS:** What does she want?

**MARTA:** She is going into the city on the weekend, so she will bring some of the blankies for the children's hospital there. Oh, and I need more money for yarn.

**CARLOS:** I'm glad you found something to occupy your mind.

# SCENE 27: MARTA IS IN DANGER

**CARLOS:** Fuck you and your dessert. "People change" . . . Go fuck yourself far from here! You! Mel . . . Maybe you two go back to that shitty life you had, with nothing . . . How about that?

**MARTA:** Carlos, please!

**CARLOS:** I will let you go! Go! Do what you want. Run with the fucking wolves . . .

*CARLOS grabs MARTA by the neck.*

But if you leave, don't come back! Let's see how you survive. What will you do? With no degree . . . Work in the café? You're not twenty years old anymore, Marta. Look at you!

*MARTA reacts, defending herself.*

**MARTA:** Carlos, stop, you're hurting me.

**CARLOS:** You will learn this time.

# SCENE 28: THE LAST DANCE . . .

*This scene is the climax of a love story, full of pain and disappointment . . .*

*MARTA and CARLOS dance, exploring tango movements together. As they dance, we hear their voices through voice-over. Between their dialogue, the voice-over of women survivors of domestic violence continues, each woman saying her name and giving her testimonial.*

**CARLOS:** *(voice-over)* Marta cooked a special dinner.

**VOICE-OVER:** Maria da Penha. He shot me while I was sleeping. Now I'm paralyzed from the waist down.

**MARTA:** *(voice-over)* I'm tired.

**CARLOS:** *(voice-over)* Marta is wearing a beautiful dress and an apron.

**VOICE-OVER:** Linda dos Santos. He destroyed my self-esteem.

**MARTA:** *(voice-over)* I still remember the first time Carlos beat me.

**CARLOS:** *(voice-over)* It's just another day.

**VOICE-OVER:** Diana Romero. I escaped in the middle of the night.

**MARTA:** *(voice-over)* I don't feel safe in my own home.

**CARLOS:** *(voice-over)* Marta wants to feel pretty.

**VOICE-OVER:** Amanda Rose. He burned my nipples with a cigarette and all of my face with hot water.

**MARTA:** *(voice-over)* I trusted him.

**CARLOS:** *(voice-over)* Beautiful smile.

**VOICE-OVER:** Ana Soares. He said that I couldn't survive without him.

**MARTA:** *(voice-over)* I feel embarrassed.

**CARLOS:** *(voice-over)* Marta was wearing a red dress.

**VOICE-OVER:** Chelsea Thompson. He broke all of my teeth.

**MARTA:** *(voice-over)* I loved Carlos.

**CARLOS:** *(voice-over)* Marta laughed at Carlos's jokes.

**VOICE-OVER:** Caroline Sullivan. I survived eighteen years of abuse.

**MARTA:** *(voice-over)* He raped me more than once.

**CARLOS:** *(voice-over)* Marta likes to dance.

**VOICE-OVER:** Ruth Thomas. He said he would kill me and all my family if I said anything.

**MARTA:** *(voice-over)* I lost count of how many times Carlos said, "This is not going to happen again. I love you."

**CARLOS:** *(voice-over)* They became husband and wife.

**VOICE-OVER:** Andrea Clark. I thought maybe that's the way he loves me.

**MARTA:** *(voice-over)* I wish I had never met Carlos.

**CARLOS:** *(voice-over)* Where is that woman I met?

**VOICE-OVER:** Dai Nakamura. I lost my vision with a punch.

**MARTA:** *(voice-over)* I want to get my life back.

**CARLOS:** *(voice-over)* You're my wife.

**VOICE-OVER:** Vanessa Garcia. He broke my cellphone. The police said, "Make out with your husband, he probably needs more sex."

**MARTA:** *(voice-over)* I thought he would change.

**VOICE-OVER:** Laura Hall. He puts his gun to my head in front of our son.

**CARLOS:** *(voice-over)* You're a piece of shit.

**VOICE-OVER:** Sarah White. Nothing compares to being afraid of dying at the hands of the person you love.

**MARTA:** *(voice-over)* I want to feel loved.

**CARLOS:** *(voice-over)* You have to do what I say.

**VOICE-OVER:** Antonella Matarazo. I was kept hostage in my own house.

**MARTA:** *(voice-over)* I can't look at myself in the mirror.

**CARLOS:** *(voice-over)* What are you going to do?

**VOICE-OVER:** Karen Duff. He choked me until I passed out.

**VOICE-OVER:** COVID-19 lockdowns around the world brought a rise in domestic violence.

**MARTA:** *(voice-over)* I'm scared.

**CARLOS:** *(voice-over)* Look at you!

**VOICE-OVER:** Cortney Lee. Every three minutes, every five minutes, every ten minutes, women's bodies are found.

**MARTA:** Marta leaves the house.

**VOICE-OVER:** Marta Dias.

*The song and movement/dance comes to an abrupt halt.*

MARTA *leaves the house.* CARLOS *is stunned.*

*Blackout.*

*Thanks for reading . . .*

# ACKNOWLEDGEMENTS

Thank you to the Canada Council for the Arts, ArtsNL, White Rooster Theatre, Neighbourhood Dance Works, Playwrights Atlantic Resource Centre, and the City of St John's.

Hailing from Brazil, Vanessa Cardoso Whelan is a playwright, multidisciplinary artist, street performer, and clown with a passion for contemporary theatre and body movement awareness, especially related to Flamenco dancing. Graduating in Theatre Arts in 2004, she has performed with several artistic groups on stage and in street productions as an actress, Flamenco dancer, puppeteer, and fire-flow dancer. Vanessa has been actively engaged in the local arts scene since moving to Newfoundland in 2014. She likes to give her art back to the community, doing volunteer performances for new Canadians/ refugees and non-profit organizations. Because of that and other achievements, Vanessa received the 2023 Inspiring Immigrant Woman Award from the We Care Foundation. Always inspired by nature, Vanessa loves the mountains on the west coast of Newfoundland. It reminds her of home.